NATIONAL GEOGRAPHIC

T0045282

I Can Breathe Underwater

Pat Malone

I walk to the edge of the sea.

The sand is cool under my feet.

The water is cold.

I put on my mask.

I put the snorkel in my mouth.

I go underwater.

It works!
I can breathe air on land
and underwater!